CW01651924

Whe… ’s Away the Mice will Play

A play by Susan Akass
Illustrated by Michael Reid

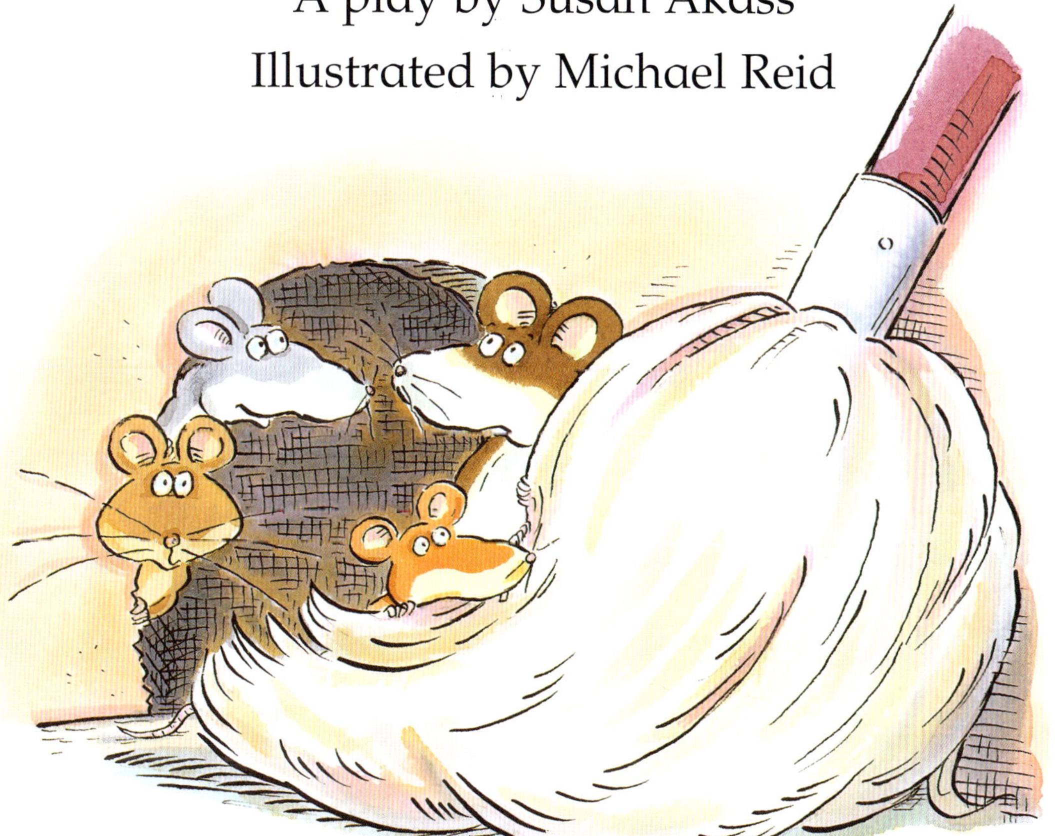

Characters

Mrs Green

Puss

Beady

Whiskers

Twitch

Nibble

Scene One

Mrs Green: Puss! Puss!

Puss: Miaow!

Mrs Green: Come on, Puss, get into your basket.

Puss: Miaow!
I don't want to get in there.

Mrs Green: Got you, Puss!

Puss: Miaow!

Mrs Green:	Time to go to the cat show. Let's put on your ribbon.
Puss:	Miaow! I don't want to go.
Twitch:	What's that miaowing?
Nibble:	It's Puss.

Beady: Mrs Green has put
Puss in the cat basket.

Puss: Miaow!
Let me out!

Whiskers: He doesn't like it!

Beady: They're going out.

Twitch: Come on!
Now we can go out and play.

Nibble: Mmm!
Now I can find some cheese.

Scene Two

Beady:	Look at me! I can swing! Up and down! Up and down!
Whiskers:	Look at me! I can slide! Wheee! Down I go!
Twitch:	Look at me! I can roll! Round and round! Round and round!
Beady:	What are you doing, Nibble?
Nibble:	I'm looking for cheese.

Twitch:	I want to swing now, Beady.
Beady:	Come on then, Twitch. Can I go on the slide, Whiskers?
Whiskers:	Yes, and I can roll now!

Beady:	We can play all day. Puss is away!
Twitch:	Don't you want to play, Nibble?
Nibble:	No, I'm looking for cheese.

Scene Three

Mrs Green:	Here we are, Puss. Back home.
Puss:	Miaow!
Mrs Green:	Good Puss. Come out of your basket.
Puss:	Miaow! Back at last.

Scene Four

Twitch:	What was that?
Whiskers:	I don't know.
Beady and Twitch:	Oh no! It's Puss!

Twitch: Puss is back!
Run!

Whiskers: Run, run, run!

Beady: Don't stop, Nibble. Run!

Nibble: But I've found some cheese.

Nibble:	Ow! My tail! Help! Help!
Whiskers:	Oh no! Look at Nibble!
Beady:	His tail is in a trap!
Twitch:	Come on, let's help him.

Whiskers, Twitch and Beady: Pull! Pull! Pull!

Mrs Green: Eek! Mice!

Puss: Miaow!
I can't see any mice.

Mrs Green: Look, Puss!
Up there, behind you.

Puss: Where?

Mrs Green: *There!*

Whiskers, Twitch and Beady: Pull!

Nibble: Ow! My tail!

Sunny Flakes
FLOUR
PUSS

Puss: Now I see them.
Yum! Yum!
Here I come!

Twitch:	Your tail is out, Nibble. Run!
Beady:	Run!
Whiskers:	Don't look back, run!

Mrs Green: Go on, Puss, get him!

Puss: Miaoooow!

Puss: Miaow!
I missed!